GROUND RULES

GROUND RULES

100 EASY LESSONS
for GROWING *a*
MORE GLORIOUS
GARDEN

KATE FREY

TIMBER PRESS · PORTLAND, OREGON

Published in 2018 by Timber Press, Inc.
The Haseltine Building
133 S.W. Second Avenue, Suite 450
Portland, Oregon 97204-3527
timberpress.com

Printed in China

Text design by Hillary Caudle
Cover design by Mia Johnson

33614081365578

ISBN 978-1-60469-878-7

Library of Congress Cataloging-in-Publication Data

Names: Frey, Kate, 1960- author.
Title: Ground rules: 100 easy lessons for growing a more glorious garden / Kate Frey.
Description: Portland, Oregon: Timber Press, 2018. | Includes
    bibliographical references and index.
Identifiers: LCCN 2018024164 | ISBN 9781604698787 (hardcover)
Subjects: LCSH: Gardening.
Classification: LCC SB450.97 .F73 2018 | DDC 635—dc23 LC
    record available at https://lccn.loc.gov/2018024164

Catalog records for this book are available from the
Library of Congress and the British Library.

Introduction

Some of us are born with a talent for gardening; others come to gardening later in life. Whether you're experienced or a novice, there is much to learn in order to be able to create and maintain a successful garden. This book contains 100 essential "rules" for you to discover and use. It's my hope they will steer you toward success at every step and help you avoid mistakes.

Successful gardens are healthy, thriving places that lift us up and create joy. They are places where practicality and aesthetics are wedded. A garden must work well within its local conditions and the framework of your life. Gardens form an important link with nature and the changing seasons—the cycle of life. Many studies have shown time spent in nature benefits us by lowering stress levels and making us feel better emotionally. A garden that focuses on plants rather than

hardscape like pools, decks, and patios can be an extension of nature. Gardens give us the satisfaction of creating and tending a special place with our own hands. They are places where we both give and receive. Imagine sweet fragrances wafting, soft leaves rustling in the breeze, shade on a hot afternoon, and an ever-changing array of flowers embroidering the yard. Imagine too the joyful songs and forms of bright yellow goldfinches against the clear blue sky, a velvet-upholstered bumblebee on a purple salvia, butterflies like snips of tapestry, and hummingbird duels over crimson blooms—all elements of life you have enabled. Gardens can be your own personal paradise.

This book is divided into six complementary sections that take you from the very first planning stages, through the joy that plants bring, soil and its important underground processes, how to be wise with water, how to be a good garden parent, ways to invite wildlife into your garden, and finally to creating a garden of earthly delights. Taken as a whole, it offers a system of practices and design considerations that address every aspect of gardening.

This is a distillation of what I have learned through my many years of gardening and designing gardens professionally in the United States and around the world. It is an effort to engage everyone with the many pleasures gardening offers. I love the subject more and more each day, and I hope you will too.

PLANNING YOUR PARADISE

This lovely scene is the result of careful planning for look and function. It illustrates a variety of seating areas, screening, pathways, and transitions from one level to another. A variety of plants soften the hardscape and tie everything together.

Become your own garden designer.

Developing a basic garden design is relatively simple. First, consider the necessities of access to the front door, front yard, and backyard. Make paths wide enough for two people to walk side by side. Decide where they begin and end. Do you like straight lines or curves? The journey should be as beautiful as the destination. Do you want privacy or an open front yard that all can see? You can screen or filter the view with plants, not just fences. Is there a place for a fountain, bird bath, or bench? Access to the backyard should be large enough for transporting materials, wheelbarrows, and other necessities. Think about a seating area or patio big enough for tables and chairs. Do you want a lawn for kids to play on? Surround it with planter beds. Where should the vegetable garden go? Some people like it far away, others near the house. Planting beds against the house or by fences or sheds can enhance, hide, or screen them. What do you want to see when you look out the window? Using hoses, landscape flags, lines of flour, or spray paint, mock up locations of paths, seating areas, and beds—live with them, then make necessary changes before beginning the work.

The plants in this exuberant composition, *Salvia* 'Caradonna', *Penstemon* 'Garnet', yarrow, lavender, and *Verbascum nigrum*, look great together and thrive because they share the same needs— drought resistance, low soil fertility, and a situation with full sun.

Make a list of plants or colors you like.

Harmonious gardens use plants that look good together. Select plants complementary in color and form, with compatible needs. For example, if you like purple foliage, begin with something like a 'Grace' purple smoke bush (*Cotinus* 'Grace'). It does best in full sun, is drought resistant, and doesn't need highly fertile soil. Add crimson autumn sage (*Salvia greggii*), red hot pokers (*Kniphofia* species), garnet or deep purple penstemons, the single red rose 'Alatissimo', pale yellow sunroses (*Helianthemum* species), and silver dusty miller for a traffic-stopping combination. Use this approach for whatever color or plant combination appeals to you. But remember: the best gardens are those with plants that are appropriate to and reflect your local area.

Plan for a long season of interest.

Include plants in your garden that bloom early, mid, and late season.
Bulbs are great additions for early spring blooms. Crocuses, fawn lilies,
scillas, snowdrops, and grape hyacinths are all lovely early garden subjects and return year after year. Plants like Lenten roses (*Helleborus*
species), daphnes, sarcoccocas, and manzanitas (*Arctostaphylos*
species) bloom early in the year and are very low maintenance, with
foliage that always looks good. Midspring and summer contain too
many plants to list, but fall plants need mention. California fuchsias
(*Epilobium* species) put on a spectacular show, as do many salvias like
S. greggii, *S. splendens* 'Van Houttei', 'Waverly', 'Amistad', 'Anthony
Parker', 'Phyllis Fancy', 'Indigo Spires', and 'Mulberry Jam'. (Many
late-blooming salvias are hardy only in mild areas but can be grown as
annuals in cold climates.) Asters are great plants for the fall garden and
there are selections for every climate. A gorgeous white aster is 'Monte
Cassino' (*Symphyotrichum pilosum* var. *pringlei* 'Monte Cassino'). 'Lady
in Black' aster (*Symphyotrichum lateriflorum* 'Lady in Black') has dark
foliage that looks great all season.

This singing symphony of color uses flowers in a variety of pink hues and enhances its impact with the addition of the blue-purple and white lupin.

Get sophisticated with color.

Gardens composed of plants with similar color harmonies or hues, rather than just primary colors, tend to be easier on the eye and our sensibilities. Beware of planting mostly red, blue, and yellow flowers— they tend to look glaring outside very large areas (like in front of palaces or in public parks) where they are appropriate in relation to the space. Instead, sprinkle primary colors sparingly throughout a composition of harmonious hues to add sparkle to the overall effect. For example, a planting of mostly pink flowers can be sprinkled with a few magenta or deep raspberry flowers, such as knotweeds (*Persicaria* species), and crimson flowers to add zing to the whole ensemble.

The silvery leaves of lambs ear and artemisia radiate light and beautifully
illuminate purple salvia blooms, creating an uplifting scene.

Gray is gorgeous.

Gray is a color as much as green. Particularly in areas where summer drought is common, this is a color to embrace. There are many
beautiful, striking plants with gray, silver, or white foliage, and many
are drought resistant. Some outstanding choices are dusty miller
(*Jacobaea maritima*), lavender, artemisia, silver vernonia (*Vernonia
lindheimeri* var. *leucophylla*), *Salvia* 'Pozo Blue', *Achillea* 'Moonshine',
silver-edged horehound (*Marrubium rotundifolium*), ajania (*Ajania
pacifica*), rose campion (*Lychnis coronaria*), curry plant (*Helichrysum
italicum*), lamb's ears (*Stachys byzantina*), lavender cotton (*Santolina
chamaecyparissus*), Russian sage (*Perovskia* species), and blue oat
grass (*Helictotrichon sempervirens*), to name just a few. Gray foliage
reflects the heat of the sun, cooling the plants. Some gray plants have
leaves covered with fuzz or hair, which breaks up air currents and
keeps the leaves from losing too much moisture. Gray foliage is won-
derfully versatile and combines well with white, purple, pink, red,
orange and pastels.

Each leaf on these coleus, hosta, croton, and dogwood (clockwise from top left) is a painting. They will highlight a planting wherever you place them.

Use variegated foliage for visual zing.

Variegated foliage has a special, appealing quality. These beautiful leaves come in many colors and patterns beyond plain green, and can be decorative features in themselves. As foliage lasts the entire growing season, their distinctive beauty is enduring. The variegation itself can be white, chartreuse, yellow, orange, or burgundy. Many plants with variegated foliage are not as strong as those with all-green foliage because the part of the leaf that can photosynthesize is smaller. They also sunburn easily and should be sited accordingly. As valuable as they are, it's easy to overdo variegated plants in the garden. Variegated leaves create a busy picture. A few sprinkled here and there makes a greater impact than many massed together. They often look great in containers.

Colors dance lightly through this mingled garden. And when plants like the purple poppy are finished blooming, you will hardly notice the spent flowers and foliage.

Go mingle.

Some people like to plant multiples of the same plant in swaths or blocks; others prefer a more mingled, impressionistic effect. The disadvantage of planting in swaths is that when a plant is out of bloom, the area it occupies won't look great, and might be downright unsightly. With a more mingled planting, if one plant is out of bloom, it won't be that noticeable as the area is small and hidden among current blooms. To make your garden look like an impressionist painting, plant in groups no bigger than three.

Plants can transform even the smallest space into a
place of joy, while also supporting wildlife.

Design a plant-centric garden.

Gardens are essentially about plants, not hardscape, but our gardens
have to be a balanced combination of them both. We need to get from
here to there in our gardens and also have a place to sit and enjoy
the view. Not everyone can afford big hardscape elements like decks,
extensive paved walkways, pools, patios, living walls, or living roofs.
The good news is, most of us can afford plants. An abundantly planted
garden is friendly to wildlife and a joy to the gardener. If we learn
how to propagate plants, whether by collecting seeds, taking cuttings,
or dividing and replanting, one plant becomes many, and our gardens
become more profuse. Extra plants make a perfect gift to friends and
are a simple way to share happiness.

Be lavish with containers.

Containers are like living flower arrangements, offering endless opportunity for wonderful color combinations. Their mobility, along with the huge range of plants they can hold, makes them an essential element in any garden. They can feature tiny succulents, riotous annuals, profuse perennials, and even small shrubs and trees. Let your imagination run wild—create combinations that complement both the pot and the garden and that delight the eye. If you combine several different plants in a single container, use a pot that's big enough and be sure they all have similar requirements for light, moisture, and feeding.

These dwarf conifers create a deeply textural, interesting scene all year long—and have the same water and soil fertility needs.

Understand your shrubs.

Shrubs come in many shapes and sizes and have different aesthetic personalities. Some are evergreen, others deciduous. Some have showy flowers or fruits. All have an individual beauty that can be brought out with judicious training and pruning. Get to know a shrub's size, shape, bloom time, and specific needs before you purchase, plant, and prune it. Above all, think about what you want your shrub to *do*. Will it be part of a mixed border? A hedge? A single specimen? Does it need to look its best at a particular time of year? Books and online information can help.

Think carefully about paths.

Paths are an important garden design element, so it pays to give them serious thought. Do you prefer straight lines or curves? Straight paths carry us rapidly to our destinations, both physically and visually. We take in our route all at once. Straight paths create a strong sense of order, control, and purpose. They work well in formal landscapes, or if there is a focal point as a destination. Curving paths are dynamic and operate like water—they capture and carry us along in their currents. To create real flow, they should be wide enough for at least two people to walk side by side. Create pools and eddies for benches or seats and vignettes of interest to captivate and hold a viewer in place. Shrubs placed at curves can partially obscure the view—if you have enough room, design paths that curve out of sight to generate a strong current that pulls visitors along.

Surveying the world from the sanctuary of a bench under a
plant adorned trellis makes us feel comfortable and safe.

Pay attention to enclosure and openness.

We respond differently to a space depending on whether it's
enclosed or open. Too much cover is oppressive; on the other hand,
we can feel vulnerable in a completely open garden. The protective
roof of a tree canopy, an overhanging trellis, or an overhead arbor all
generate feelings of comfort and calm. Looking out on an open area
from a semi-enclosed space energizes us and lifts our spirits. We
feel safe but, anticipating what we might encounter, develop a keen
interest in what is outside our shelter.

THE
JOY
OF
PLANTS

Mosses, irises, and azaleas, all adapted for shady, moist conditions, combine naturally to make a lovely, distinctive garden.

Plant what works.

All plants have evolved in specific climates, exposures, and soil types. Of course, many common landscape plants are fairly forgiving about the conditions they grow in—that's why they're common. But plenty of plants are more particular. You'll find that many plants adapted to shady sites will burn in full sun. Likewise, plants adapted to sunny, dry sites will likely die in shady, moist conditions. Some plants need deep, nutrient-rich soil with a high organic matter content. Others thrive in areas with rocky, nutrient-poor soils. The moral is—get to know your site. Look up your weather patterns, dig a hole to determine your soil type and its depth, and watch each part of your garden throughout the day and seasons to learn the patterns of sun and shade. Then do your homework: if there's a specific plant you want to grow, look up its requirements before you buy it. Impulse buying can lead to disappointments.

RULE

14

Feed high-nutrient-requiring plants like roses each
year with organic fertilizers and compost.

Meet your plant's specific needs.

In many gardens, and particularly around older houses, you may
want to preserve existing plants even though you plan to make
many changes. Just as humans have specific nutritional needs, so do
plants—your final plan may include plants with very different nutrient needs. Plants with high nutrient requirements, such as roses or
camellias, can be catered to by simply putting a big circle of good
compost around them each year for added fertility. This leaves you
free to grow less-demanding plants in other parts of the garden.

Don't buy rootbound plants.

It's an unfortunate fact that nurseries sometimes sell plants that aren't in peak condition. Plants that have been in the pot too long will have tightly packed roots, and most do not recover well when planted, especially annuals, trees, and shrubs. In particular, woody plants are apt to develop "circling" roots, which can strangle the plant long after it's in the ground. Don't buy these plants. Instead, select one where the roots just fill the container.

For good value, look for perennials in one-gallon pots like these.

Start small.

Plants grow best when planted small. You may be tempted by a large, mature plant at the nursery, but smaller, younger plants become established much more quickly. In fact, studies have shown that smaller sizes of the same plant catch up with larger specimens within a remarkably short time. Trees and shrubs adapt to a site most easily when planted from a one-gallon or five-gallon pot, rather than a ten-gallon, fifteen-gallon, or larger size container. Perennials and annuals are best planted from four-inch to one-gallon pots. You may have to wait a bit, but the results will be worth it!

Plant at the right time.

In hot, dry, summer climates, such as in the Southwest and California, it's best to plant in the fall or very early spring. Fall-planted plants will have strong root systems by the spring and grow fast as the soil warms and the days lengthen. In harsh winter climates (the upper Midwest, New England), plant as early in the spring as possible so plants have a chance to get settled in and grow roots before the summer heat begins. However, keep in mind that frost-sensitive plants, including many annuals and vegetable crops like tomatoes, shouldn't be planted until all danger of frost is past and the soil has warmed up.

This impressive California lilac flourishes in warm regions but would perish in a cold New England winter.

Go native.

Native plants adapted to your local conditions will thrive, look natural, and attract wildlife. But be aware that all plants have evolved with specific soil types, exposures, and climates. Plants from rocky areas need to be planted in well-drained soils, while plants from riparian areas will likely need moist conditions and fertile soil. Plants from the mountains often have a hard time growing in low, hot valleys. Prairie plants perform best in deep, loamy soils. Hardiness is also an issue. Make sure to select native plant varieties from your area. Get to know your region and the native plants. Native plant nurseries usually provide good cultural information and are happy to talk about the plants they grow.

Site size matters.

One of the most common mistakes is to put a plant in a space or container that it will ultimately outgrow. In a container, plants can quickly become rootbound and won't thrive. Trees and shrubs sited in a too-small space will require regular pruning to keep them in bounds. This takes time and generates prunings you'll need to dispose of. It makes much more sense to simply site plants where they can grow to their ultimate height and width with minimal pruning for shape. Nursery labels usually give a plant's ultimate height and width. Believe them!

Buy local.

Large chain stores and nurseries often have a buyer who is not familiar with local conditions. The plants offered for sale at these outlets may not be cold hardy or adapted to your climate or soils. Local nurseries, especially those that propagate their own plants, are usually very knowledgeable about plants and more familiar with local conditions and the plants that thrive there. Often the owners and staff are delighted to share their experience.

Remedies for poorly drained soils include digging in
compost and planting things like black-eyed Susans.

Compost to the rescue.

Poorly drained and compacted soils are common around houses.
These problems can occur naturally, but frequently soils are compacted during the home construction process. In housing subdivisions,
topsoil is often scraped off and, after the homes are finished, trucked
back in and applied on top of the compacted subsoil, creating very difficult growing conditions. Plant roots and soil organisms need oxygen
just as much as we do, and as these soils are so tightly packed, there is
little available. To promote better drainage in such extreme conditions,
initially you'll need to dig in large amounts of compost—at least a four-
to six-inch layer. After a season or two, you can just spread nutritious
material like composted greenwaste as a mulch. Another way to cope
with this condition, at least initially, is to use plants that can tolerate
poor drainage, such as ornamental grasses, roses, figs, black-eyed
Susans, and ornamental creek dogwoods (*Cornus sericea*). See rules
30–43 for more on how to care for soil.

RULE

22

Succulents are a popular drought-resistant choice
and look appropriate in dry conditions.

Choose water-wise plants.

If you live in a part of the country with low or sporadic rainfall and
limited water availability, it just makes sense to choose plants that are
adapted to those conditions. These plants employ a variety of mecha-
nisms to avoid water loss. Among them are white, gray, or silver foliage;
hairy stems and leaves; resinous, waxy or leathery leaves; reduced leaf
size; shedding leaves during dry spells; and dormancy during times of
drought. Many plants combine a number of these survival strategies.
Another good reason to choose drought-adapted plants in dry areas—
besides the obvious advantage of saving water—is that these plants *look*
right in those conditions, whereas a lush, bright green plant will seem
out of place.

RULE

23

Annuals like calibrachoas, blue honeyworts, marigolds, and
love-in-a-mists (clockwise from top left) sing with loud voices,
devoting their lives to flowering in many forms and colors.

Grow amazing annuals.

While perennials are often treated as the stars of the garden, annuals have much to offer: a profuse and long season of bloom, dazzling colors, and (usually) easy care. But the word "annual" is something of a misnomer—most annuals live for a season, not one year. So-called hardy annuals are somewhat frost tolerant and grow best in cooler seasons. Tender annuals grow in frost-free times of year and thrive in warm weather. Annuals need consistent water and friable, fertile soils to grow rapidly and bloom profusely for the longest time possible. Remove spent flowers for a longer bloom and protect plants from slugs and snails. Dwarf annuals often lack the vigor of their full-size counterparts. If you want to grow annuals in a pot, make sure it's at least five gallons. Group several pots together for a brilliant show, and keep the plants deadheaded for longest bloom.

Waiting a second year for bloom is a small price to pay for
the spectacular beauty of these Canterbury bells.

Learn the secrets of biennials.

Biennials include some wonderful plants but are underused because
many gardeners don't understand how they grow. As their name
suggests, biennials complete their life cycle in two years—the first
year only leaves are produced, with flowers appearing the second
year. After a spectacular flowering, they die and you'll need to replant.
Stunning biennials include Canterbury bells (*Campanula medium*),
sweet Williams (*Dianthus barbatus*), mulleins (*Verbascum* species),
and (in milder areas) tower of jewels (*Echium wildpretii*). Biennials
can either be set out as young plants in spring or early fall or sown
directly where you want them to bloom. The extra effort to grow
them is well worth it.

Graceful miscanthus glows with fall color, creating a warm and relaxing scene.

Choose the right ornamental grasses.

Grasses can be a wonderful addition to your garden, but it pays to be choosy. They can be evergreen or winter dormant, large or small. Large, perennial, deciduous grasses like miscanthus are hard work to cut back in winter and generate a large amount of plant debris. Some grasses seed profusely; others not at all. A number of perennial grasses (and their lookalikes, the sedges) are smaller, evergreen, and easy to combine with bulbs and small perennials. *Acorus* and *Carex* species, and grasses like giant feather grass (*Stipa gigantea*), prairie dropseed (*Sporobolus heterolepis*), woodoats (*Chasmanthium latifolium*), pink muhly grass (*Muhlenbergia capillaris*), feather reed grass (*Calamagrostis* ×*acutiflora*) and some fountain grasses (*Pennisetum* species) are much easier to care for. Grasses are generally deer and insect resistant. Their presence in the landscape softens and relaxes it.

RULE

26

Depending on how carefully you prune, wisteria can grow into a delicate tracery or it can gobble your whole house.

Choose vines wisely.

Vines add a welcome vertical green and flowering accent to the garden—but beware! Many are vigorous, and some are rampaging monsters. They range from seasonal annual vines like sweet peas, to robust perennial climbers like sweet autumn clematis (*Clematis terniflora*), which can grow to thirty feet. Some, like Japanese honeysuckle (*Lonicera japonica* 'Halliana'), should be avoided at all cost because they're horribly invasive and impossible to eradicate. Fortunately, there are many lovely, well-behaved honeysuckles such as American honeysuckle (*L. ×americana*) and trumpet honeysuckle (*L. sempervirens*). Wisteria is an extremely vigorous but rewarding vine that needs yearly pruning. And clematis are divided into groups, each of which has different pruning requirements. Provided you do your research, you're sure to find the perfect vine for every situation.

Spring-blooming snowdrops signal the end
of winter and never fail to charm.

Wake up the garden with spring-blooming bulbs.

Spring bulbs are heralds of life. Every year we delight in the first blooms when much else is dormant. Best planted in the fall, they reward us year after year, blooming early then ceding the stage to their summer-blooming garden neighbors. If sited between winter-dormant perennials, their spent leaves will be covered by growing foliage as the season progresses. Some examples of early bloomers are fawn lilies (*Erythronium*), grape hyacinths (*Muscari*), crocus, scillas, snowdrops (*Galanthus*), leucojum, and reticulated irises. These are followed by daffodils (*Narcissus*), fritillaries (*Fritillaria*), and tulips. In mild areas (USDA Zone 8 and warmer), you can grow exotic beauties like ixias, sparaxis, ranunculus, and freesias.

RULE

28

Alliums are a perfect place to start
experimenting with summer bulbs.

Bulbs are for summer, too.

Gardeners tend to forget there are bulbs that bloom in summer. Best planted in fall or very early spring, these bulbs are wonderful for tucking between herbaceous perennials when they are cut back or haven't fully grown yet. Many summer bulbs have tall and narrow flowering stems. When blooming, the flowers can hover above lower-growing perennials, making a lively picture. As the perennials' foliage grows it supports the bulb stems and hides their sometimes unsightly lower leaves. Good examples to try include alliums or onion flowers, with their lollipop heads; lilies of all kinds; gladioli, either the big ruffled hybrids or the simple species; and crocosmias, which come in a wide range of sizzling colors.

Clockwise from top left: dwarf iris, sparaxis,
species tulip, fawn lily (*Erythronium*).

Defy the dry with drought-tolerant bulbs.

Some bulbs are adapted to a dry-summer climate and can get by with
little or no irrigation. These are good choices where water is limited—
they can transform areas that would otherwise be bare to scenes of
beauty. Many bulbs native to the arid West and the Mediterranean
are in this category and include bulbs like calochortus, brodiaeas,
erythroniums from the western United States, dwarf irises, lycoris,
narcissus, anemones, leucojum, scilla, freesias, Spanish hyacinths,
grape hyacinths, ixias, sparaxis, wild tulip species, and many alliums.
Celebrate your dry climate by planting some of these spectacular
spring- and fall-blooming bulbs.

THE
REAL DIRT

Be kind to your soil.

Your entire garden depends on soil for its life, so it makes sense to
nurture it as much as possible. Depending on what plants you grow,
your soil should have an organic matter content between 6 percent
and 10 percent. If you grow plants like annuals, vegetables, and those
(like roses) requiring rich, fertile soils with high amounts of organic
matter, spread a one- to three-inch layer of compost or mulch on top
of the soil each planting season. Spreading a layer like this is often just
called mulching and is different from digging in or tilling. Perennials
and trees should be mulched with compost once yearly. All plants,
even cacti and succulents, benefit from compost—though these need
small amounts infrequently.

Be a soil scientist.

Plants have preferences and dislikes for various soil textures, and you'll be much more successful if you make your plant choices accordingly. Soil is composed of sand, silt, clay, or loam (a combination of the first three). Sandy soils have large particles, drain quickly, and are not very fertile. Silt soils are composed of small, flat particles and compact easily. Clay soil particles are even smaller and can form very heavy soils that drain slowly but tend to be very fertile. Loam—the mixture of all three textures—is best for most plants. How can you figure out what's in your garden? Dig a shovelful of soil and look closely at the texture—is it crumbly or dense? That's your first clue. Then add a bit water and make the soil into a ball with your hand. Clay and silt soils hold together, sandy soils fall apart. Loam soils will also fall apart, but slowly. And voilà—you'll be better prepared for your next trip to the nursery or garden center.

Pay attention to soil structure.

Good soil structure is essential to growing healthy plants. The good news is, it's far easier to influence soil structure than texture. Well-structured, or friable, soils are porous, so oxygen and water can move through. (Plant roots and soil organisms need oxygen as much as we do!) An ideal soil structure resembles the crumbly aspect of a good chocolate cake and takes time to achieve. The best way to do this, depending on the quality of your soil, is to either mulch with compost or dig it in. For loamy soil, mulching is often all you need to do. With compacted, heavy clay, or sandy and infertile soil, you will want to initially dig in about four to six inches of compost (if you're trying to grow a vegetable garden in this situation, you may need to dig in compost for three to five years). As structure develops (think crumbly cake), you can simply mulch. The build-up of organic matter from compost nurtures the microorganisms, soil fungi, earthworms, and other organisms that are essential to building soil structure. Observe your soil over time and watch it happen!

Figure out your soil profile.

What you see on the soil surface doesn't often indicate what's underground. Soil depth is vital to plant roots. The best soils are very deep and have good texture and porosity so plants roots can penetrate deeply. Many soils are shallow, or have underlying clay, making it difficult or impossible for your plants' roots to grow deep. Soil depth is difficult to change but can be improved over time by mulching with a coarse-textured compost that earthworms and other soil organisms will breakdown, eat, and incorporate. To determine your soil's depth, simply dig a hole two feet deep with a posthole digger or shovel and see what the cross-section looks like. If it turns out your soil is shallow, be especially careful when selecting trees. You'll have more success with trees that have shallow, fibrous roots, like the smaller maples, rather than deep-rooted species.

RULE

34

Take a break! Mulching develops soil structure and health better and more easily than tilling or digging.

Spread it, don't till it.

Though it may seem counterintuitive, mulching with compost or composted green waste increases your soil's organic matter content much faster than tilling it in. This is because earthworms and other soil organisms are very efficient at incorporating organic matter into the soil. Studies have shown that frequent tilling increases the oxygen content in the soil so much it causes organic matter to decompose very quickly, and its benefits are partially lost. The only time it makes sense to till is if you have heavy clay, sandy, or compacted soil. In this case, an initial tilling of about four to six inches of compost into the soil will break up compaction, help clay soils to drain, and allow sandy soils to retain moisture. Then you can transition to no-till. All plants grow beautifully with this method.

Nurture your roots.

Most plant roots are in the top foot of soil. The area where roots grow
is called the rhizosphere, and is teeming with life. Roots produce
substances known as exudates, which promote specific soil organisms
according to the plant's need for nutrients and disease suppression. If
you want a healthy, productive garden, create a healthy rhizosphere
over time by adding organic matter from compost. Mulching and
keeping disruptions to a minimum is best for most gardens (Put away
that tiller!), but in cases where soil is compacted, heavy, or sandy, initially tilling in compost can help develop better structure more quickly.

Ditch those landscape fabric weed barriers.

Plastic or fabric landscape cloth laid over soil for weed control creates a physical barrier that prevents organic matter from nourishing the soil. Also, it's not very good at suppressing weeds! For effective weed suppression, use corrugated cardboard during the rainy season and cover it with three to six inches of compost. (For more on using cardboard, see rule number 70.)

Don't fertilize everything the same way.

Some plants, such as vegetables, many annual plants, flowering perennials, roses, and some shrubs and trees need high soil fertility. Others, such as those from desert or mountain regions and sandy or gravelly, nutrient-deficient soils, grow best in low-fertility soils. Adjust your compost and fertilizer additions accordingly. Plants with low-fertility needs are best nourished with small amounts of compost, not fertilizer. For plants with higher needs, use compost plus organic fertilizers, which release their nutrients over time so are effective for a longer period.

Make high-quality compost.

Compost is made from different ingredients and has varying nutrient levels. The essential ingredients are plant organic matter (soft-textured leaves, plant trimmings, grass clippings, straw) and manures. The best compost has a balanced carbon-to-nitrogen ratio. Carbon comes from coarse organic matter like yard clippings, leaves, or straw. Too much carbon, especially very coarse or woody materials like sawdust or wood shavings, creates nutrient-deficient compost. Nitrogen comes from ingredients like lawn clippings, manures, and legumes like alfalfa, clover, vetch, peas, or bean plants. Make sure to include both carbon- and nitrogen-rich materials in your compost pile. (It's easiest to mix all ingredients together rather than trying to create a "lasagna" pile, where each ingredient is put in a strict layer.) Your pile needs to be well aerated, since the composting process requires oxygen. The carbon-rich coarse ingredients help bring oxygen into the pile, as does turning it. You can turn your pile with a garden fork each week or two (which will hasten the composting process) or simply let it sit for several months. The result will be the same—dark, crumbly, sweet-smelling compost.

Give your garden a tea party.

Compost tea is great stuff—it can supplement nutrients, boost soil organism levels, and suppress leaf diseases. It can be sprayed directly on plants or on the surrounding soil. The quality of the tea depends on the quality of the compost you use, as well as on the tea-making process. Although you can buy compost tea, lots of gardeners enjoy making it, and there are plenty of instructional videos online.

RULE

40

Among other benefits, mulch can provide a
beautiful backdrop for greenery.

Embrace mulching.

Mulch is a plant- or manure-based material placed on the surface of
the soil. A good, nutritious mulch is basically coarse compost. It can
be made from composted green waste, plant waste, and manures.
(Green waste is a good-quality compost produced by many munici-
palities from plant debris collected by homeowners and landscapers.)
The texture should be just coarse enough to appeal to earthworms,
but not so fibrous or coarse as to rob nitrogen from the soil as it
decomposes—beware of compost with large chunks of tree bark in
it (bark mulch contains very few nutrients). Mulch acts to suppress
weeds, protect the soil from the drying effects of the sun, and help
develop soil structure. It also increases soil fertility as it breaks down.
As an additional benefit, it can cover drip irrigation lines and protect
plants from rain splash. It is both an attractive cover on the soil and
an essential element for healthy gardens.

Not all mulches are equal.

Some mulches are attractive but not beneficial to soil. Shredded and ground bark mulches are among the worst, as they never break down to add nutrients. Woodchip mulches are popular, but as they break down, the microorganisms that decompose them rob nitrogen from the soil. As a result, plants grown in these soils are nutrient starved and don't grow well or look good. The only place where woodchips are appropriate and beneficial is under mature trees, which generally require lower amounts on nitrogen than other plants.

Fungi are your friends— invite them in.

Mycorrhizal fungi are soil-dwelling fungi that have mutually beneficial associations with most of the world's plants. They aid in the uptake of water and nutrients like phosphorus and help plants to resist drought by expanding their root systems. In fact, they're so effective that many tree nurseries inoculate their stock with mycorrhizal fungi. Various formulations of mycorrhizal fungi are available for the home gardener. They're most useful in soils that have nothing growing in them or have been highly compacted from construction. Before you buy, check the label: the more species in the formulation, the better. Simply dust it on your plant's roots when planting.

Don't forget about your containers.

The commercial potting soil used in containers and planting boxes is intentionally designed to drain quickly. Fast-draining soil is highly porous, so nutrients move through it very quickly, which can lead to your plants' becoming starved. The remedy is to apply fertilizer monthly. An excellent organic fertilizer ingredient is feather meal (made from ground chicken feathers). It's most effective during the warm months, and releases its nutrients gradually. One application lightly dug into the soil lasts two to three months. Topping containers with compost is also highly beneficial, since the plants get fertilized every time you water.

BE WISE WITH WATER

This stylish, water-wise garden matches drought-tolerant
heuchera and pennisetum with gravel instead of a lawn.

Think carefully about how your garden uses water.

Water is a precious substance, and will only become more so as our climate continues to change. In planning your garden, and in choosing plants, think about how much water they will need. If you can find ways to reduce your water consumption, such as mulching or reducing the size of your lawn, implement them. Also, take cues from your climate—it's foolish and wasteful to use extravagant irrigation to try and turn your yard into something it was never meant to be.

Plants that share water needs, like these agave and barrel cactus, make happy companions.

Learn to hydrozone.

Hydrozoning is the simple practice of grouping together plants with the same water needs. It makes your garden easier to tend and keeps your plants happy. If you have an automatic irrigation system, plants with similar needs should be in the same station or sprinkler zone so you can adjust irrigation duration and timing to their specific requirements. If you water by hand, hydrozoning makes the task a lot simpler. Even in areas with regular rainfall, annual plants and some perennials and shrubs will need supplemental water during dry spells.

Help keep streams and rivers clean.

Cultivating healthy soil has some surprising benefits for your local ecology. As it turns out, the actions of healthy soil and plant roots help to purify water as it filters into the ground. The creatures that live in healthy soil, including microorganisms like bacteria and fungi, act to break down not only organic matter but pollutants as well. Plants help take up nutrient excess before it infiltrates groundwater or flows into streams and rivers. They also help capture sediments—one of the main pollutants of our waterways.

Boost your plant's yield and appearance with drip irrigation.

Make your plants happy and your life easier—and save water too! Studies have shown that drip irrigation results in higher plant yields by as much as 24 percent. It also applies water exactly where you want it, limiting waste. And as a bonus, minimizing the moisture area also minimizes the ability of weed seeds to germinate and grow. Drip irrigation is also useful for containers where summer rainfall is not regular.

Get on the grid.

When you put in a drip irrigation system, create a grid with a consistent distance between lines. This makes it simple to locate lines under a layer of mulch. When you find one line, you will know where all the others are. When you add a plant, do so at the existing drip line. You can use a line with no drip emitters (called a blank line) and pop in drippers as needed, or use emitter tubing, which comes with drippers spaced at regular intervals in the line. With emitter tubing, you won't have to pop in any drippers and irrigation coverage in your garden bed will be consistent.

Be smart about where the drip emitter goes.

For a newly planted plant, the drip emitter should be directly next to the root ball—otherwise you risk having it dry out and die in the summer heat. As plants mature and roots grow out, they are better able to seek water from drippers farther from the main stem. With trees, the original drip emitter can be plugged as the tree grows and you add more drippers further from the trunk. With containers, use circles of quarter-inch emitter tubing (spaghetti tubing) to wet the whole pot—a single dripper on one side of the pot will only water part of the root ball, stunting growth or even killing the plant.

Don't mix delivery systems.

Each type of water delivery system—sprayers, drip emitters, quarter-inch soaker dripline (emitter tubing or spaghetti tubing), and drip tape—puts out differing amounts of water per hour and operates at different water pressures. Many people don't realize this and mix water delivery systems in the same area, with the result that each part of the garden gets vastly different amounts of water. Spray systems put out the most water in the shortest amount of time and can deliver many gallons per hour, depending on the size of head, water flow, and pressure. Drip emitters typically deliver water at the rate of one-half gallon per hour (0.5 GPH), 1 GPH, or 2 GPH and typically work best at 30 pounds per square inch (PSI). Drip tape waters at about 0.63 GPH and works at pressures of 4 to 12 PSI. If you have a large planter bed or your garden is on a slope, make sure to use pressure-compensating (PC) drip emitters so plants at the beginning and end of the line get the same amount of water. Spaghetti tubing (quarter-inch dripline) works at lower pressures, is semi-pressure compensating, and puts out between 0.5 and 1 GPH, depending on water pressure. It is the perfect easy choice for containers, small raised vegetable boxes, and small or irregular planters.

It's all in the timing.

Whether you're dealing with a lawn, vegetables, flowers, or containers, plants grow best with a regular water supply. It's all too easy to forget to turn water on or off—not to mention what happens when you go on vacation. There are all kinds of timers that can help keep your watering consistent—hard-wired electronic timers, solar-powered timers, and very convenient battery timers that screw onto a faucet. Be sure to adjust your timers seasonally or when the weather changes.

Water containers and raised planters often.

Because potting mixtures drain quickly, plants in containers and raised beds will need watering more often than plants in the ground. In hot, dry weather, small containers may need watering every day. A good way to check to see if you need to water is to stick an old screwdriver or your finger in the soil to see if it's moist. If it's dry, water well. With containers and smaller raised boxes, spaghetti tubing is often the easiest way to water. Putting them on a timer for consistent water will keep them looking good.

HOW TO
BE A GOOD
GARDEN
PARENT

Regularly removing spent flowers like the ones on this cosmos will keep them blooming all season long.

Deadhead spent flowers for additional bloom.

Get out your pruners! Removing spent flowers often stimulates additional bloom. The flowering stems of herbaceous plants can be cut back individually as they fade, or all at once to promote strong, new, lower growth. Some perennials, such as lungworts, yarrow, and hardy geraniums, will even regenerate completely when cut to near the ground after bloom. The new foliage is fresh and attractive, and usually stays that way the rest of the season. One hint: don't leave gawky, leafless stems—cut them back to a cluster of leaves or the base of the plant for a more pleasing, natural look.

Cut back herbaceous plants at the end of the season.

Many herbaceous plants need cutting back at the end of the growing season. Often fresh, young growth appears at the base, indicating the need to cut the old foliage to this point. Other plants can be sheared or cut back by half or more and remain evergreen over winter. Lavenders, autumn sage (*Salvia greggii*), and other semi-shrubby perennials just require their spent flower stems to be sheared off. Tracy DiSabato-Aust's invaluable book, *The Well-Tended Perennial Garden,* describes these techniques and each plant's requirements in detail.

Save some seed heads for the birds.

Standard garden practice has traditionally been to do a thorough tidying-up in the fall. But many gardeners—particularly those who advocate the use of native plants—now recommend seed heads and dead plant stalks be left standing for the winter because they provide food and shelter for birds and beneficial insects. It may look a bit scruffy for a couple of months, but the benefit to wildlife is considerable. Plus many seed heads look beautiful with frost or snow on them. If you choose to go this route, wait until late winter—just before new growth starts—to do your garden cleanup.

RULE

56

Wallflowers offer several years of beauty
before they need to be replaced.

Some plants are beautiful but short-lived.

Don't worry—it's not you! It's just the way the plant is constituted.
Lavender and wallflowers are common examples—lavender lives from
five to ten years, while wallflowers may be at their best for only two
or three years. Hummingbird mint (*Agastache* species), another very
worthy plant, lives about one to five years. And many gardeners find
that purple coneflowers begin to decline after several years. All are still
worth including in your garden because of their floriferous beauty and
long bloom duration. Simply replace them when they decline.

Make more plants.

Some perennials and ornamental grasses develop bald spots in the center of the clump after they've been growing for a few seasons. This indicates that they need to be divided. Otherwise, new growth will occur only at the margins of the clump, and the plant's overall vigor will decline. Cutting the clump into several pieces and replanting them will reinvigorate the plant and, as a nice bonus, will give you more plants! Dig up the clump, then use two digging forks (if the root ball is large) to pry the clump into pieces, or cut it up with a spade or shovel. If the clump is small, you can use an old kitchen knife (be careful!). For particularly large, tough root balls, such as those of some ornamental grasses, you may even need to use a saw. Replant only those pieces that have vigorous-looking growth; discard the bald parts. Some plants are best divided in spring, others in fall. Check a good reference guide to see which is best for the plant you're dividing.

For a (relatively) weed-free garden, don't let a single weed go to seed.

Weeds can easily take over a garden—and if you let them go to seed, you'll be locked into a frustrating cycle of endless weeding. Pull out weeds, root and all, as soon as you can after they appear. This is often easiest when the soil is somewhat moist in spring. Over time, this will result in a weedless garden. Diligent time spent on this task now will pay off for years to come.

Don't plant too high.

Keep roots in the dark. When you put a plant in the ground, make sure it's at ground level—not above it with roots exposed to the sun. Potting soil is designed to drain quickly, so if part of the root ball is above the soil level in the garden, the plant will dry out faster than the surrounding soil and will either fail to thrive or die. Cover the root ball at time of planting with one-third inch of native soil to keep it at the same moisture level as the surrounding soil.

Plant trees for shade and coolness.

Trees provide many benefits to an environment, whether urban, suburban, or rural. Urban and suburban areas can be seven to seventeen degrees warmer than surrounding rural areas due to the effects of heat captured by and radiated from pavement and buildings. That's why dense, urban areas are sometimes referred to as "heat islands." Trees, shrubs, and other greenery can greatly ameliorate this effect by casting shade, decreasing water evaporation, and limiting heat radiation. A shady garden is a welcome sanctuary during hot summers.

Not all trees are as easy to accommodate as this small dogwood, which, with its lovely blooms, fits easily into a garden and allows for planting beneath.

Pick the right tree.

Before you buy a tree, do some homework. A tree can be a lifelong investment in happiness—or a headache. Make sure it's adapted to your conditions, the mature size will suit the site you have in mind, and the required maintenance is acceptable. Some trees are short-lived and decline after twenty-five years, while others can live for several hundred. Some trees, like elms, beeches, or maples, have thick surface roots or cast deep shade, and it's difficult to grow anything under them. Others, such as crab apples and ginkgoes, are easy to plant under. Some trees generate tremendous amounts of litter, like acacia and mimosa. If you're willing to do the cleanup, great—but don't fool yourself into thinking that a messy tree will take care of itself. Word of warning: reject any tree that's rootbound (you'll have to partially remove it from the nursery pot to check). The roots should fill the pot nicely but not appear congested. If the roots are circling around the inside of the pot, don't buy the tree.

Protect young trees from sunburn with latex paint.

Give your tree some TLC.

Caring for your tree begins right after you bring it home from the nursery. First, dig a hole that's wide enough to easily fit the roots. It only needs to be as deep as the diameter of the root ball, and you don't need to amend the soil in the hole. Be careful not to cover the base of the trunk with soil. Second, many young trees with thin bark, such as maples, can sunburn, especially on the west side—the problem is exacerbated if trees are drought stressed. Until their bark thickens (usually in a few years), paint it with white latex house paint. Third, young trees benefit from a nutritious mulch on soil at all times. Finally, thin up crowded branches and limbs (as appropriate) as they grow.

Grow trees from seed.

Oaks, buckeyes, hickories, pecans, black walnuts, and other large-seeded trees grow readily from acorns or nuts planted in situ (outside in the ground), which allows their taproot to grow uninterrupted. Though aboveground growth is slow the first year, root growth is extensive. Trees planted in situ from seed grow rapidly and establish quickly. And growing trees from seed gives you a wonderful sense of accomplishment.

Well-pruned trees have a natural beauty.

Prune tree branches the right way.

Trees naturally develop a healthy root/shoot/leaf ratio, and so should be pruned only for a specific purpose. A properly pruned tree looks natural. If you find that you need to remove a branch, you may be tempted to just cut if off where you want to, rather than considering the tree's natural form and character (a practice known as "heading"). Don't. This kind of cut is harmful to the tree's viability and structural integrity, especially when it's done to a mature tree. It's best to completely remove unwanted or nuisance branches down to a lower branch junction rather than head them.

When removing a branch, cut to the collar.

When you need to remove a tree branch, make your cut right above the "collar" or "wrinkle"—the slight swelling at the base of the branch between the branch and the trunk. This kind of cut will heal rapidly. There is no need to apply paint to the surface of the cut—in fact, this can impede healing.

These Japanese maples are pruned to enhance their natural shape, making them lovely additions to the garden.

Prune shrubs to preserve their beauty.

Turning shrubs into "lollipops" destroys their character and is hard to correct. Not only do lollipop shrubs require frequent pruning, they also forfeit the potential for natural beauty. Before pruning, observe how the plant grows, and consult a good book. For a natural shape, thin branches as needed and to enhance the existing structure. If you want to put small plants or a groundcover under the shrub, you can remove some of the lower branches.

The vigorous willows pictured here are pollarded each year as a form of art. Many trees are pruned this way for no reason, and are far more beautiful when allowed to grow naturally.

Say no to plant torture (pollarding).

Pollarding, popular in Europe, is the practice of pruning the main branches of a tree or shrub to the same place each year, producing a gnarled knob at the end of each branch. In winter, this gives the tree a surreal artistry, and in summer they have a rounded crown of dense, bushy growth. Here in the United States, it is often done to trees to keep them at a specific height. Our crape myrtles, fruitless mulberries, and sycamores are often victims of this practice. In most situations, it looks highly artificial, is expensive, generates large amounts of pruning waste, and can weaken the plant over time. If not done for a specific reason, it's completely unnecessary—trees should simply be thinned as needed to open up their natural structure.

Treat your roses right.

With their sumptuous flowers and often heady fragrance, roses are understandably popular. Yet their need for proper pruning and fertile soil also makes them widely misunderstood. The wood on many shrub roses loses vigor after one to five years—renew it by simply sawing off the failing branch at a low branch junction. Remove a couple of branches each year or two to keep shrubs strong. This stimulates fresh, robust growth. For a long season of bloom, remove spent flowers—a technique known as deadheading. With climbing roses, create a permanent scaffold of branches by selecting healthy, well-placed shoots, then renew secondary wood every one to three years. Many roses are grafted, and will throw off suckers from the rootstalk. These should be removed promptly. If you can find ungrafted roses—known as "own-root roses"—you won't have to do this. All roses need highly fertile soil and regular water. Give them a thick addition of nutritious compost each spring, along with an application of organic fertilizer, which will provide a sustained dose of nitrogen.

Give your garden a makeover.

When you move into a new house, or just decide the garden needs renovation, how do you choose what goes and what stays? First, look at the plants. If you see some that are weedy, like privet or tree of heaven, or that are obscuring a pathway or important view, or just aren't thriving, consider taking them out. You may simply not like some plants, or they may not contribute to the scene you envision. Those can go, too. The trees and shrubs you want to keep may have become overcrowded and need thinning. Finally, look at what's left and add a selection of plants that combine well visually and have the same needs as those you've decided to keep. If you have limited room, consider carefully. Maybe a shrub is not bad, but you would really prefer something fragrant like a daphne. If you have a white-blooming crape myrtle or a silver pear, select plants that complement those colors. Maybe you only have spring-blooming plants and need some summer color. Include salvias for summer and fall interest, and for the hummingbirds. Add a fall-blooming, fragrant, rough-leaf hydrangea (*Hydrangea aspera*). You'll be amazed at the transformation.

RULE

70

Clumps of dirt can help weigh your cardboard down when you initially lay it out. Once you've got it where you want it, cover it completely with compost.

Cardboard to the rescue.

When starting a new garden, or recapturing a weedy existing garden, sheet mulch with corrugated cardboard to kill the weeds. It's easy: just cover the weeds with a single layer of cardboard, and then top the cardboard with three to six inches of compost. This will both smother weeds and build healthy soil. In addition, earthworms love the cardboard and will eat it and lay eggs in it, tilling the soil for you. Cardboard needs moisture to break down, so for a weed-free bed, do this in fall or two to three months before planting in early spring.

Control destructive critters.

Each part of the country has its own critter problems. In the Northeast and central United States, it's woodchucks (and often rabbits and squirrels). In the Northwest, it's moles. In California, it's gophers. And just about everywhere, it's deer. Different animals need different control methods. For smaller animals (such as woodchucks and gophers), trapping can be effective (but check the laws in your area regarding the trapping of wild animals—you may not be allowed to transport them off your property). For larger animals, such as deer, installing a fence may be the only truly effective deterrent (it's also possible to achieve a measure of success by planting deer-resistant plants). Your local university extension program website will have useful, tested information on how best to deal with problem animals.

Repot when necessary.

Plants in containers often decline in vigor and appearance over one or more years as they become root-bound. When this happens, they need replanting into a larger container or into the ground. A five-gallon container is the smallest size to use for just about everything besides succulents. When replanting into another container, use one that's at least four or more inches larger to allow for new root growth.

RULE

73

These yellow rudbeckias, though joyful now, may be a problem later on.

Watch out for the spreaders.

Some attractive garden plants spread over time and should be carefully sited with this in mind. (Hint: when you're buying plants, be alert to the words "spreads" and "vigorous" in the descriptions.) It may take several years before this tendency is revealed. A sure sign is shoots coming up far from the mother plant. Perennial sunflowers, slender vervain (*Verbena rigida*), Mexican evening primrose (*Oenothera speciosa*), Griffith's spurge (*Euphorbia griffithii*), some monardas, some ornamental oreganos, plume poppy (*Macleaya cordata*), some asters, and Korean bellflowers (*Campanula takesimana*) are all spreaders.

Though English ivy, purple loosestrife, pampas grass, and
Japanese barberry (clockwise from top left) can be attractive
in gardens, they are a real threat to native wildlife.

Never, ever plant invasives!

Plants that escape into the wild can be devastating to the environment.
Every responsible gardener should check his or her state list of invasive species. Keep in mind that just because a plant isn't invasive in one
region that doesn't mean it's not invasive in another with a different
climate. Some of the most widespread invasive plants include English
ivy (*Hedera helix*), butterfly bush (*Buddleia* species), Japanese barberry
(*Berberis thunbergii*), purple loosestrife (*Lythrum salicaria*), Oriental
bittersweet (*Celastrus orbiculatus*), and pampas grass (*Cortaderia
selloana*).

BIRDS,
BEES,
AND
BUTTERFLIES

This redbud has gorgeous flowers in spring that
bees visit. Later, birds eat the seeds.

Plant a garden of life, for life.

Being in a garden with a profusion of foliage, flowers, and animated, living creatures is an experience that stays with you forever. Plants are both enablers and manifestations of life, and when the space around them hums with flitting hummingbirds, swiftly darting bees, and butterflies with tapestry-like wings, we come alive as well. Gardens that support life with wildlife-friendly plants are gardens that give to all.

Welcome in the good guys.

For us, flowers are a source of beauty. But many beneficial insects require flower nectar as a food or energy source. As adults, hoverflies, lacewings, and parasitic wasps feed only on nectar. Their larvae are carnivorous and help control insect pests. No garden is pest free—gardens need a healthy pest/predator ratio for predatory insects to survive—but prevention is the best approach to pest control. For a resilient garden, include a lot of plants (one or two will have little effect) that offer nectar for predatory and beneficial insects. Some of the best choices are plants that have short, easily accessible floral nectar tubes like fennel, alyssum, celery, parsley, cilantro, dill, bishop's flower (*Ammi majus*), white lace flower (*Orlaya grandiflora*), purple coneflower (*Echinacea purpurea*), blazing star (*Liatris* species), black-eyed Susan (*Rudbeckia* species), mountain mint (*Pycnanthemum* species), yarrow (*Achillea* species), and small-flowered members of the daisy family like calico aster (*Symphyotrichum lateriflorum*). Many native shrubs also make good choices.

Aphids like soft, succulent foliage and may be a natural occurrence in your spring garden, but if they persist, it may mean your plants are stressed.

Don't stress your plants.

Stressed plants emit compounds that are attractive to pest insects. So don't let that happen! Common sources of stress are drought, poor soil fertility and structure, climatic incompatibility, or excessive use of chemical fertilizers. Insecticides aren't the answer—they kill both pest insects and beneficial insects, and the pests will rebound much more quickly. Instead, mitigate stress by paying attention to soil quality, proper siting, and adequate irrigation.

Be a friend to the bees.

It's a happy coincidence that a bee-friendly garden is a flower-filled garden. Bees are the world's most efficient pollinators, and they need consistent, diverse, and abundant pollen and nectar. Pollen, composed of proteins, minerals, and fats, is primarily a larval food. Nectar is composed of sugars and is the daily fuel for adult bees. Many bees practice flower constancy, which means, in the course of one day, they visit the same species of flowers again and again. To make life easier for them, provide patches of each type of flower that measure at least three by three feet, or repeat the same type of flower through-out the garden. And plant lavishly—it takes about one acre of flowers to support just one colony of honeybees. Good choices among annuals include sunflowers, bidens, cosmos, poppies, cilantro, basil, viper's bugloss (*Echium* species), and phacelias. Among perennials, choose lavender, rosemary, catmint, calamint (*Calamintha* species), asters, oreganos, purple coneflower (*Echinacea purpurea*), anise hyssop (*Agastache* species), penstemon, pincushion flower (*Scabiosa* species), goldenrod (*Solidago* species), and blanket flower (*Gaillardia* species). Keep in mind that the pollen and nectar in double flowers such as roses, camellias, and dahlias may be inaccessible.

A native blueberry bush not only makes a great hedge but also provides a feast for you and your garden's avian visitors.

If you need to plant a hedge, go native.

Often when it comes to planting a hedge, we fall back on the usual suspects: yew, boxwood, arborvitae, and so on. But these plants offer little value to wildlife. A hedge of native shrubs can provide privacy and define garden space just as well as those old standbys with the added benefits of: pest control, bird habitat (who doesn't love watching fledgling birds grow up?), and food for pollinators, to mention just a few. With so many advantages, what's not to like?

RULE

80

Salvias are a good choice for attracting
both butterflies and bees.

Embrace the joy of diversity.

Including a diversity of flowering plants and shrubs will help invite
a diversity of life into your garden. The flowers of many plants cater
to more than one organism. For example, many plants with flowers that support beneficial insects also support bees. A number
of butterfly-attracting flowers also support hummingbirds. The
caterpillars of many butterflies and moths can only feed on specific
plants—growing a wide variety, especially natives, increases the odds
that you'll be able to satisfy their appetites. Flowering plants are
good for birds because of the number of insects they attract—over
93 percent of birds feed their young on insects. Flowering plants
also provide structural complexity for perching and nesting, as well
as seeds, fruits, and berries to nourish birds throughout the year. Of
course, another benefit of diversity is that it allows you to revel in
the glorious variety of garden plants available to us!

Provide water for wildlife.

Bees, frogs, toads, and birds all need regular, clean water. Honeybees use water to cool the hive during warm weather. Birds, both resident and migratory, need regular and clean water to drink and to bathe in. Sometimes more birds visit a bird bath than do a bird feeder! Toads and frogs, which are efficient predators of pest insects, need water to lay eggs in and for tadpoles to mature—watching them develop is one of the great pleasures of having a pond. To provide for tadpole needs, the pond should be at ground level and free of fish and chlorine. It should measure at least six by six feet, and be one and a half feet deep or more, depending on the climate (colder climates require greater depth). If you're worried about mosquitoes, you can control them with biological mosquito floats. Water, in whatever form, is a life-saver for wildlife.

An iridescent green *Osmia* bee contrasts
beautifully with a purple penstemon.

Provide a habitat for native bees.

Astonishing but true: there are an estimated *four thousand* species of native bees in the United States. (Honeybees are not native—they were imported by European colonists.) And they're fascinating creatures. Most are solitary, not social. Approximately, 70 percent nest in burrows in the ground, and 30 percent nest in crevices of wood or hollow plant stems like raspberries or elderberries. Native bees co-evolved with certain plants—they are active in the part of the season in which those plants are blooming and only live above ground as adults for about six weeks. Each bee species visits preferred plants. Male native bees sleep in or on flowers and can't sting. Unfortunately, because of habitat loss, many native bees are in decline, and some are feared to be extinct. Our gardens can help them survive—don't fear them, welcome them!

Become a bumblebee watcher.

They're cute and charismatic. And they're actually better pollinators than honeybees! Bumblebees are an example of social native bees. The queens form seasonal colonies. At the end of the season, the old queen dies and new queens overwinter in the ground or in plant debris. Bumblebees need consistent floral bloom during their season of activity. For the most part they prefer the flowers of perennials, shrubs, and trees, but they're also essential for pollinating tomatoes, eggplants, blueberries, and cranberries. In spring the queen emerges from hibernation and finds a place to nest, at which point she needs access to spring- and summer-blooming plants. At the end of the season, to build up reserves for winter, the queen turns to late-flowering plants such as goldenrod, asters, flowering oreganos, salvias, catmint (*Nepeta* species), calamint (*Calamintha* species), heleniums, eupatoriums, sedums, perennial sunflowers (*Helianthus* species), and blue mist shrub (*Caryopteris* species). As with other native bee species, many common bumblebees are declining due to habitat loss and introduced pests and diseases. Help them out!

Beneficial insects like this lacewing will protect your garden better than any pesticide.

Don't use pesticides.

Pesticides of any kind, whether synthetic or organic, are highly detrimental to all bees and beneficial insects. There is no safe way or time to use them. For a thriving garden, develop a healthy soil, practice the "right plant, right place" approach, and include flowers to support beneficial insects. If a plant keeps getting attacked by pests, remove it and replace it.

By incorporating favored shrubs and trees and, of course, a birdbath, backyard birders can enjoy lively scenes like this songbird pool party.

Make your garden into a haven for birds.

Some birds live in our gardens year-round; others are temporary visitors, overwintering or nesting in them, or simply migrating through. At all times birds need food, shelter, perching sites, and water. Some birds dwell in forests, others in grassland, and some in a mix of both. It's well worth consulting a book or website on how best to provide for your local birds' needs. Bird activity and song are the most charming and soothing sounds we can surround ourselves with, and yet many of our most common songbird populations are declining due to loss of habitat. Life in our gardens is something that affects us deeply—we should do everything in our power to help it thrive.

A goldfinch prepares to feast on the seed
head of a purple coneflower.

Don't cut down those
seed heads in fall.

The seed heads of perennials such as coreopsis, coneflowers, sunflowers, and rudbeckias are an important food source for chickadees,
cardinals, nuthatches, sparrows, towhees, goldfinches, and many other
birds. In fact, goldfinches are among the only birds that feed seeds to
their young, nesting later in the summer for this purpose. The song
of goldfinches is among the most cheerful of any songbird, and their
brilliant yellow forms collecting seeds from flowers are like paintings
on the wing. Don't deprive them of the food they need!

Native North American honeysuckle will brighten
your garden and feed happy hummingbirds.

Help the hummingbirds— join the nectar highway.

Most hummingbirds migrate to Mexico and South America for the winter. (An exception is the Anna's hummingbird, which now lives year-round in the western United States.) During migration, hummingbirds follow a "nectar highway" of blooming native plants that cater to them. We can help them on their migrations or nesting by including plants they feed on in our gardens—many of these are favorites with humans as well thanks to their showy flowers. Some of the best choices include salvias, bottlebrush and red buckeye (*Aesculus parviflora* and *A. pavia*), hummingbird mints (*Agastache* species), grevilleas, honeysuckles, columbine, monarda, heucheras, butterflyweed (*Asclepias tuberosa*), Joe-Pye weed (*Eupatorium* species), zinnias, aloes, fairy dusters (*Calliandra* species), erythrinas, justicias, and California fuchsia (*Zauschneria* species).

Joe-Pye weed is a favorite of swallowtails and other butterflies.

Plant a butterfly nectar garden.

What would a garden be without butterflies? If we want them to come, we need to offer them nectar-rich flowers. And not just any flowers: butterflies will only sip nectar from specific plants, particularly those that secrete nectar at the bottom of floral tubes, which butterflies can reach with their long proboscis. Favorite and easy-to-grow nectar plants include echium, centranthus, verbena, Joe-Pye weed, phlox, lantana, ageratum, blue mist flower, milkweed, and salvias such as bog sage (*Salvia uliginosa*). Most butterflies only live from two to six weeks. The exceptions are butterflies that migrate, such as monarchs, which can live for about five months, and those like pipevine swallowtails that overwinter as adults.

Feed the caterpillars.

Each species of butterfly caterpillar feeds on a specific group of plants. Keep in mind that caterpillar host plants may be different from the ones the butterflies visit for nectar. If you want to attract butterflies, it makes sense to include host plants in your garden. Many swallow-tail caterpillars feed on members of the carrot family, which includes native species as well as fennel, parsley, dill, and other familiar plants. Monarch caterpillars feed only on milkweeds (be sure to plant milk-weed species that are native to your region—not the tropical *Asclepias curassavica,* which may disrupt monarch migration patterns and serve as a host for harmful protozoans). Another example is the gorgeous pipevine swallowtail, whose caterpillars feed only on members of the genus *Aristolochia,* commonly known as Dutchman's pipes. Include this living gem in your garden.

A GARDEN OF EARTHLY DELIGHTS

Discover the joy of nurturing plants.

Plants represent life. They give us oxygen, shade, food, fuel, and building material; they reduce pollutants and feed our animals. And above these critical but utilitarian needs, plants form the basis of our connection with nature. The resinous scent of a fir tree, the joyous yellow of sunflower blooms, the buzz of bees wallowing in poppy flowers—these sensations lower our stress levels and make us happy. Caring for a garden enables us to create a small world and watch it grow and change over seasons and years. We can rejoice in the clove-like fragrance of honeysuckle in the evening, welcome birds as they appear, and have dinner with our families under the swaying leaves of a tree we planted. In creating a place for others, human and wild, we care for ourselves too. Few activities give such a feeling of lasting accomplishment as making and tending a garden with our own hands. Gardening yields both a material and an inner harvest.

Don't just read about nature—experience it.

Reading about monarch butterflies is very different from watching the caterpillars grow. They start out as tiny dashes of greenish-white and soon become fat, brilliant green-and-yellow-striped eating-machines demolishing milkweed leaves. Then they transform into an emerald chrysalis beaded with shimmering gold—a wonder of design. Ten to fourteen days later the chrysalis turns dark, and a seeming miracle of brilliant orange and black emerges and unfolds its wings. To witness this process is to experience the essence of life. These dramatic events exist all around us—we just need to invite them into our gardens by including plants that support them. Start with planting native milk-weeds for monarch butterflies and watch the magic begin.

RULE

92

Yellow roses, pink foxglove, and purple geraniums
mingle with joyful abundance.

Lift your spirits with a profusion of flowers.

A garden in which plants are separated by oceans of cement, mulch,
or gravel, or in which plants play a minimal role, is much less emotionally moving than a profusely planted garden with an abundance of
flowers. Most English gardens are planted so that foliage and flowers
intermingle, whereas many American gardens seem to have adopted
a do-not-touch rule—a kind of social phobia that vastly diminishes
flower power. Plant profusely and feel happy.

Bellflowers and hydrangea help give this all-white
garden a long and beautiful bloom.

Go big and long with color.

Color is emotional. Profuse color makes our hearts sing. Color is also
subjective—we all have favorite colors and combinations we choose
for our houses or clothing—but floral colors have a universal appeal.
Virtually all of us respond positively to both brightly colored and
pastel flowers. Even all-white gardens can be stunning. Some flowers
have a very long bloom season. These colorful super-bloomers include
bidens, zinnias, petunias, orange cosmos (*Cosmos sulphureus*), verbe-
nas, catmints (*Nepeta* species), blanket flowers (*Gaillardia* species),
agastaches, cupheas, penstemons, yarrows (*Achillea* species), salvias,
Aster ×frikartii 'Mönch', bottlebrushes (*Callistemon* species), fuchsias,
flowering maples (*Abutilon* species), and hydrangeas. Include at least
some super-bloomers in your garden for easy color all season.

Revel in voluptuous fragrance.

Fragrances have an incredible ability to evoke nostalgia and create atmosphere. There are many different types of scents: sweet, light, heavy, spicy, citrusy, musky. Some are exotic, others familiar; some drifting, others detectable only close up. Some plants are fragrant at night, others in daytime—it depends on the habits of the pollinators they're meant to attract. It's possible to have fragrance for almost the entire growing season. For winter, consider sweet box (*Sarcococca* species), winter daphne (*Daphne odora*), early-blooming narcissus, winter honeysuckle (*Lonicera ×purpusii*), and witch hazel (*Hamamelis* species). Some spring-blooming plants are jasmine (*Jasminum* species), mock orange (*Philadelphus* species), Korean spice viburnum (*Viburnum carlesii*), some azaleas (*Rhododendron* species), lilac (*Syringa* species), and clove currant (*Ribes odoratum*). The choices for summer are many: lilies, roses, old-fashioned petunias, heliotrope, flowering tobacco (*Nicotiana* species), osmanthus, citrus, Mexican orange blossom (*Choisya ternata*), and star jasmine (*Trachelospermum jasminoides*). Fall's choices are fewer, but still captivating: katsura tree (*Cercidiphyllum japonicum*), osmanthus, and harlequin glorybower (*Clerodendrum trichotomum*).

Evoke the Mediterranean with aromatic foliage.

Resinous fragrances immediately bring to mind the sunny skies and clear light of the Mediterranean. The fragrance comes from oils contained in the plants' leaves and is particularly evident in rosemary, culinary and native sages, thyme, oregano, lavender, and some rock-roses (*Cistus* species). These oils deter herbivores from eating the plants, but also evaporate on very warm days to help cool the foliage. Their aroma can appeal to us as much as sweet fragrances. Lavender soothes and relaxes us, native sages remind us of hiking in warm parks, and, given its close association with Mediterranean cuisine, rosemary's scent brings to mind a wonderful dinner.

Learn how to create emotion in the garden.

Our emotional response to a garden depends largely on its form and
how it is planted and cared for. Naturalistic and formal styles evoke
very different reactions. A garden with broad, straight paths and
geometrically regular beds tends to generate feelings of order and
control, whereas a garden with curved paths and free-form or irregular beds is more relaxing and calming. The choice of plants also has
a profound effect. An abundance of spiky foliage can generate aggres-
sive or chaotic feelings; mounding or undulating foliage can evoke the
same feelings as a body of water. Mystery is important too. In a formal
garden, you can often see everything at once, leaving little to the
imagination. An informal garden, with curving paths, arches to walk
through, or hedges that obscure certain areas, piques our curiosity.
Repetition influences mood, as does structural layering of shrubs and
trees to create shapes and patterns of sun and shade. Flower color,
whether bright or pastel, and foliage color, whether dark, silver, or
chartreuse, also affect us. Bright colors tend to make us happy, while
pastels are soothing, and an all-white garden can feel formal and cool.

Plant a garden to build community.

My mother's front yard was a small lawn no one paid attention to and was drudgery to care for. So we killed the lawn by sheet mulching it with cardboard, installed a drip irrigation system, and topped it with six inches of good compost. We then planted mock orange, magenta old-fashioned roses, dianthus, single peonies, deep blue penstemons, clary sage, blue catmint, white and blue perennial geraniums, teucrium, resinous native sages, and white California poppies in fragrant, softly mounding profusion. First to visit were the hummingbirds and bees. Then virtually every person who walked by stopped and admired the colors and life newly suffusing the garden. People changed their walking routes to include this small front yard. The garden became a vehicle of community and social interaction for my mother, who had previously been socially isolated. Each garden holds this same potential.

Make a therapy garden.

My friend Ellen developed intractable cancer in her early fifties.
Despite treatment, her condition worsened. To lift her spirits, she had
her small front lawn taken out and replaced by a variety of colorful
flowering plants and a rustic rock border that matched the style of her
Craftsman-era house. The garden overflowed with fuchsias, flowering maples, salvias, fairywands, geraniums, and other colorful plants,
and Ellen spent more and more time sitting on the steps sipping life.
It became an informal salon where neighbors would come and chat,
where worry and anxiety softened. When Ellen could no longer sit,
she lay on a sofa looking out the windows so she could see and feel
the garden. The garden couldn't cure her, but it enriched her last days
spiritually and socially in ways that mere medical treatment could
never provide.

Bathe in nature.

Many studies have documented the positive effects of plants and nature on our brains and bodies. Even a few houseplants in an office can soothe our psyches. Being surrounded by nature lowers the heart rate and blood pressure, boosts the immune system, lowers stress hormones, and induces relaxation. These effects last for several hours to several days, depending on the individual and duration of their visit. In our gardens, contact with nature can occur every day. Immerse yourself!

Design a paradise.

Many think of gardening as a chore. This mind-set leads to gardens that are no more than utilitarian spaces occupying the front or back of houses. Their owners don't interact with them much except for needed care. But imagine an inviting, engaging space, soft with moving foliage and bright with a variety of flowers, perfumed day and night, shaded from the hot sun, graced by hummingbirds and butterflies, alive with song, and offering berries or fruits to nibble—where the rest of the world slips away and we find ourselves in a haven we have created ourselves and can enjoy every day. Our gardens, no matter how large or small, can be paradise.

Resources

Books

🌿 SOIL

Lowenfels, Jeff. *Teaming with Fungi*. Portland, OR: Timber Press, 2017.

Lowenfels, Jeff. *Teaming with Nutrients*. Portland, OR: Timber Press, 2013.

Lowenfels, Jeff. *Teaming with Microbes*. Portland, OR: Timber Press, 2010.

Stewart, Amy. *The Earth Moved: On the Remarkable Achievements of Earthworms*. Chapel Hill, NC: Algonquin Books, 2004.

🌿 WATER

Kourik, Robert. *Drip Irrigation For Every landscape and All Climates*. 2nd Edition. Occidental, CA: Metamorphic Press, 2009.

🌿 RIGHT PLANT, RIGHT PLACE

Oudolf, Piet and Noel Kingsbury. *Planting: a New Perspective*. Portland, OR: Timber Press, 2013.

Oudolf, Piet and Noel Kingsbury. *Designing With Plants*. Portland, OR: Timber Press, 1999

CARE

DiSabato-Aust, Tracy. *The Well-Tended Perennial Garden*. Portland, OR: Timber Press, 2017.

Whittlesey, John. *The Plant Lover's Guide to Salvias*. Portland, OR: Timber Press, 2014.

LIFE

Adams, George. *Gardening for the Birds*. Portland, OR: Timber Press, 2013.

Buchmann, Stephen L. and Gary Paul Nabhan. *The Forgotten Pollinators*. Washington D.C.: Island Press, 1996.

Frankie, Gordon W., Robbin W. Thorpe, Rollin E. Coville, and Barbara Ertter. *California Bees and Blooms*. Berkley, CA: Heyday, 2014.

Frey, Kate and Gretchen LeBuhn. *The Bee-Friendly Garden*. Berkeley, CA: Ten Speed Press, 2016.

Tallamy, Doug. *Bringing Nature Home*. Portland, OR: Timber Press, 2007.

PARADISE

Alexander, Rosemary and Rachel Myers. *The Essential Garden Design Workbook*. Portland, OR: Timber Press, 2017.

Ogden, Scott and Lauren Springer Ogden. *Plant-Driven Design*. Portland, OR: Timber Press, 2008.

Lloyd, Christopher. *Succession Planting For Year-Round Pleasure*. Portland, OR: Timber Press, 2005.

Lloyd, Christopher. *The Well-Chosen Garden*. New York, NY: HarperCollins, 1984.

Lloyd, Christopher. *The Well-Tempered Garden*. London: Weidenfeld & Nicolson, 2014.

Magazines

Garden Design
gardendesign.com

Gardens Illustrated
gardensillustrated.com

Gardens To Visit

Asticou Azalea Garden
3 Sound Drive
Mount Desert island, ME 04662
gardenpreserve.org

Atlanta Botanical Garden
1345 Piedmont Ave NE
Atlanta, GA 30309
atlantabg.org

Biltmore Gardens and Estate
One Lodge Street
Asheville, NC 28803
biltmore.com/visit/biltmore-house-
  gardens/gardens-grounds

Bloedel Reserve
7571 NE Dolphin Drive
Bainbridge Island, WA 98110
bloedelreserve.org

Chanticleer Garden
786 Church Road
Wayne, PA 19087
chanticleergarden.org

Chicago Botanic Garden
100 Lake Cook Road
Glencoe, IL 60022
chicagobotanic.org

Denver Botanic Gardens
1007 York Street
Denver, CO 80206
botanicgardens.org

Desert Botanical Garden
1201 N. Galvin Parkway
Pheonix, AZ 85008
dbg.org

Fairchild Tropical Botanic Garden
10901 Old Cutler Road
Coral Gables, FL 33156
fairchildgarden.org

Filoli
86 Canada Road
Woodside, CA 94062
filoli.org

Lewis Ginter Botanical Garden
1800 Lakeside Ave
Henrico, Virginia 23228
lewisginter.org

Limahuli Garden and Preserve
5-8291 Kuhio Hwy
Hanalei, HI 96714
ntbg.org/gardens/limahuli

Las Vegas Springs Preserve
333 S Valley Boulevard
Las Vegas, Nevada 89107
springspreserve.org

Longwood Gardens
1001 Longwood Road
Kennet Square, PA 19348
longwoodgardens.org

Ganna Walska Lotusland
Montecito, CA
lotusland.org

Mendocino Coast Botanical Garden
18220 North Highway 1
Fort Bragg, CA 95437
gardenbythesea.org

Magnolia Plantation and Gardens
3550 Ashley River Road
Charleston, SC 29414
magnoliaplantation.com

Missouri Botanical Garden
4344 Shaw Boulevard
St. Louis, MO 63110
missouribotanicalgarden.org

Naples Botanical Garden
4820 Bayshore Drive
Naples, FL 34112
naplesgarden.org

Portland Japanese Garden
611 SW Kingston Ave
Portland Oregon 97205
japanesegarden.org

The New York Botanical Garden
2900 Southern Boulevard
Bronx, NY 10458
nybg.org

Smithsonian Pollinator Garden,
National Museum of Natural History
10 Constitution Avenue NW
Washington D.C. 20050
naturalhistory.si.edu/butterflies

Tohono Chul Gardens
7366 N Paseo Del Norte
Tucson, AZ 85704
tohonochulpark.org

Tucson Botanical Gardens

2150 North Alvernon Way

Tucson, AZ 85712

tucsonbotanical.org

United States Botanic Garden

100 Maryland Avenue SW

Washington D.C. 20001

usbg.gov

University of California Botanical Garden at Berkeley

200 Centennial Way

Berkeley, CA 94720

botanicalgarden.berkeley.edu

Minnesota Landscape Arboretum

3675 Arboretum Drive

Chaska, MN 55318

arboretum.umn.edu

Wave Hill Gardens

W 249th Street

Bronx, NY 10471

wavehill.org

Nurseries that ship nationwide

Annie's Annuals and Perennials

740 Market Avenue

Richmond, CA 94801

anniesannuals.com

Digging Dog Nursery

31101 Middle Ridge Road

Albion, CA 95410

diggingdog.com

High Country Gardens—online or phone orders only.

Santa Fe, New Mexico

highcountrygardens.com

Prairie Nursery

W7262 Dover Court

Westfield, WI 53964

prairienursery.com

Photography and Illustration Credits

All entries are listed by rule number.

travelfoto: 67

ver0nicka: 99

Viacheslav Lopatin: 12

Vitalii Hulai: 76

withthesehands: 89

Wstockstudio: 30

Zigzag Mountain Art: 94

WIKIMEDIA COMMONS

Acabashi: 56

Index

🐝 **KATE FREY** grew up in Berkeley, California. She is a noted garden designer, eloquent advocate for pollinators, and popular garden speaker and educator. She has designed and managed such famous gardens as the organic public garden at Fetzer Vineyards. Her gardens highlighting organic agriculture won two gold medals and one silver-gilt medal at the Chelsea Flower Show in London, a rare honor for an American designer. She has worked in Japan, Malaysia and Saudi Arabia. Kate currently writes two gardening columns and her book, *The Bee-Friendly Garden*, was selected as one of the best gardening books of the year in 2017 by the American Horticultural Society. Her newest educational venture, The American Garden School, made its debut in 2017.